*Alfie Alligator*

# The Alphabet Game

Judy Hindley
*Pictures by*
Colin King

Collins

First published 1985 by William Collins Sons & Co Ltd, London and Glasgow
© text and illustrations Small World 1985

2

How to play the Alphabet Game:
On every page, there is something
to see, a funny thing to say,
something to find, or something
to do. Look for the letter –
listen for the sound.

Here are some of the sounds the
letters can make:

ACK!  BANG!  CRASH!  DING!
EEK!  FIE!  GRRR!  HO!  ICKY!
JAB!  KISS!  LA!  MMmmmm  NO!
OH!  POP!  QUACK!  RAH!  SSsssss
TUT!  UGH!  VROOM!
WHOOPS!  EX
YUCK!
ZZzzz

# Aa

Axe in the apple tree –
What else begins like that?
Ask an alligator
With an apple
On his hat.

# Bb

What can you see
That starts with 'b'?
I see three things like that –
A thing that can sing,
A thing that can sting,
And a BIG BLACK BAT –
Boo, bee! You bother me!
Scat, bat!

# Cc

Can you? Can you?
Can you do what I can do?
Can you creep along
Like a caterpillar?
Can you curl up like a cat?

# Dd

What do you do
That starts with 'd'?
What do you do, my dear?
I dance until I'm dizzy
With a daisy in my ear.

# Ee

'Ello, 'ello, 'ello –
What have we here?
Egg on the edge
Egg on its end
Egg on my elbow –
Egg everywhere!

# Ff

Fie! Fo!
There's a fly on my nose!
What other funny things
Can you see?
A frog on my foot –
A flea on my knee!

# Gg

Gooey goose gravy –
Isn't it good?
Glassful of grape-juice –
Glug, glug, glug.

# Hh

Ho, ho, ho –
How shall I be happy?
I'll hop until I'm happy –
I'll hide until you find me –
And then I'll have a hug.
Ho, ho, ho!

## Ii

"Ick!" said the Indian.
"It
is
ITCHY
in
this
outfit!"

# Jj

What do you like
That starts with 'j'?
Do you like jelly?
Do you like jam?
Do you like to jump
As high as you can?

# Kk

Here is a kite
Fit for a king!
Here is a king
In the kite-string.
Give it a kick!

(I can jump higher
than a house, can you?
It's easy – a house can't jump.)

14

# Ll

Look, look
What I can do –
Leap high –
Lie low –
Lick a lovely lolly.

# Mm

The mountaineer
Has lost his map.
What a mess!
What a muddle!
Oh, where is his Mum!

# Nn

No, no, no!
This isn't nice!
Here is a ninny
With a nut on his nose,
And a noodle on his necktie!
No, no, no!

# Oo

Odd! It's an omelette!
An omelette falling off –
And here we see an officer
With omelette on top.

# Pp

"Poo!" said the pirate
Peering at his plate of prunes.
What a picky peg-leg
Poking at his p's –
Can you find the p's?
Pickles, pears, potatoes –
Look at all of these!

# Qq

Queasy, queasy queen –
She must be feeling sick.
Tuck her in a quilt,
Quick, quick, quick!

# Rr

Rrrm, rrrm, race-track rider,
Racing for a ribbon –
ROARS around the race-track –
Rrrm, rrrm, rrrm.

# Ss

See here! Sit up straight!
Sip your soup like Mrs Snake –
SSsssss – don't slurp!
What a silly sausage!

# Tt

Tut, tut, tut –
Do you have a 't'?
I have lots of 't's –'
Tummy, toes and teeth!

# Uu

Up, up, up!
Underneath umbrella
Upset
Upside down
Making ugly faces.

# Vv

Voom, vroom!
Very fast van!
Very smashed vegetables –
Very sad man.

# Ww

Woo, woo, wild wind
Whistles round your head –
Wiggly worm
Wicked witch
Warm in bed.

# Xx

X-ray
Exit
Who's next?

# Yy

Yippee, yippee! Yellow yacht
Coming round the bend –
Happy yellow yachtsman
When the day is at an end.

# Zz

Zipping in
Zipping up –
ZZZZZZZZzzzzzz
Goodnight, my friend.

Aa Bb Cc

Dd Ee Ff

Gg Hh Ii

Jj Kk Ll

Mm Nn Oo

Pp Qq Rr

Ss Tt Uu

Vv Ww Xx

Yy Zz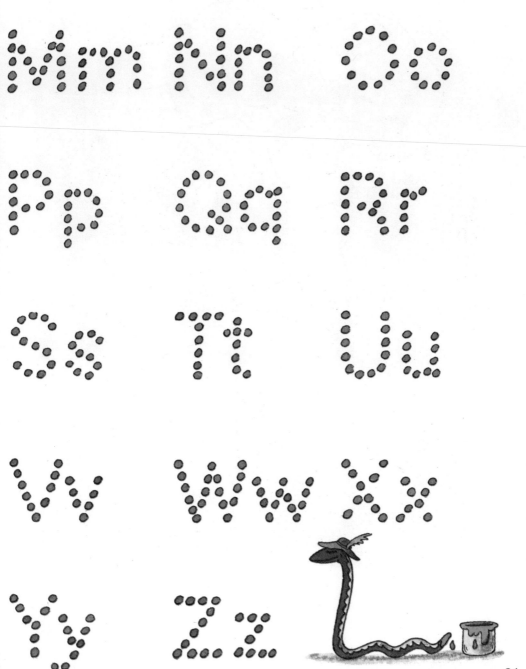